# THE SOUND OF THE LAST TRUMP

## ROBERTA RAY

# THE SOUND OF THE LAST TRUMP

**PENDIUM**
**PUBLISHING HOUSE**
514-201 DANIELS STREET
RALEIGH, NC 27605

For information, please visit our Web site at
*www.pendiumpublishing.com*

PENDIUM Publishing and its logo
are registered trademarks.

**The Sound of the Last Trump**
By Roberta Ray



ISBN: 978-1-944348-93-9

PUBLISHER'S NOTE

# CONTENTS

# PROLOGUE

Bias and coverups are the deciding factor in protecting and shielding the President from the press. I cannot imagine the fear surrounding the White House, the leaks, and leaks cause some to hide like mice, and covering for the President who only cares about himself, degrading and trashing those who are far above his character. The GOP has allowed Trump to collapse the government with conflicts and scandals, woes and woes. He cannot see his mistakes and harm caused by his own actions. He has taken so many risk and shift blame to others. The Democrats and women are his punching bags, and this impacts his staff to attack the people in a heinous way. Report after report shows that there is no regard for the First Amendment—he has branded the press as an enemy and as "fake news". The world is in chaos and being held under bondage. One Senator even classified the White House as a daycare.

# INTRODUCTION

Evangelical leaders made the choice to help elect Trump as the President. Their concern was based on removing and changing of certain laws that was made, "ETC" LGBT and ROE VS WADE, his slogans were "drain the swamp" and "Make America Great Again". Looking for justice to be served and laws to be changed after his election, his campaign began to get nasty and dirty, hurling attacks on women and attacks on his administration. Cabinet members were resigning and the election of people with troublesome pasts refilled his Cabinet. Coming into the first term of his presidency, he was met with much criticism.

The majority of his Cabinet members begin to see Trump as a thief of our democracy, and the House and Senate took to pushing their own agenda. No one called him out, they allowed him to get away with corruption, destruction and tearing down their party. They did everything they could to keep him in power and forged ahead with their own power play. Their power began to surge, they knew he would shun traditions and the policy-making process, and he relied on the advice of his friends and association interest, Sean Hannity and Laura Ingraham who were the voices in his ear. He undermined the rule of law, sadly to say, he is not in charge. Members of Congress and his own attorney, people like Mitt Mc

Connell, Paul Ryan, John Kelly, and big monies donors like the Heritage Foundation pulled the wool over his eyes. There was no checks and balances, but there are others infiltrating his cause—Nunes, Jordon, Steve Bannon, and a host of other conspirators.

President Trump's background before he ran for the office of the presidency was different from OTHER PEOPLE. He was an executive of his company. He tweets and often wiles with words, but he lacks knowledge and commitment to his own country, to the oath of office, and to the rule of law—the written law in the Constitution of the United States. He does not follow or respect the freedom of speech or the press right to published news, he always says it is fake news.

# THE CONSTITUTION

The Constitution should be defended by those who take the oath of office, and before he enters in the Executive of his office, he shall take the following OATH or Affirmation, "I do solemnly swear that I will faithfully execute the office of President of the United States, and will do the best of my ability to Preserve and Protect and Defend the Constitution of the United State. The Vice President shall be president of the Senate, and the Senate shall have the Sole Power to try all Impeachment, and the House of Representatives share equal responsibility for lawmaking with the U. S. Senate as framed in the CONSTITUTION."

# CHAPTER ONE

# THE SOUND OF THE LAST TRUMP

President Trump has given himself accolades and esteemed himself so highly. He has also built a huge statue of himself and painted it for his own trophy and use. He dances to his own music, and his own sound, he clapped and has given himself an A-plus. He has made clear his qualification and he has echoed it over and over again that no one has done what he has done. He speculates that he is the best thing that has ever happened to this nation. No other president can do what he is doing.

He said, how can you impeach someone who is doing a great job? He has repeatedly said that if he had known Sessions was going to recuse himself, he would not have put him in the office. He would have put someone else in his place. He repeated over and over that there is no collusion and he tweeted, "it is a witch hunt". He also has lied over eight thousand times and counting. He has characterized himself as being the smartest, he dismisses and retaliates against people of color and those who speak out against him, he likes to take credit for himself, not realizing someone else did it, and his endeavor is to win over hate groups.

He continues to ignite riots and stir up trouble.

# CHAPTER TWO

# What Went Wrong at Helsinki

There are many warning signs for the USA. Helsinki is the capital city and most populous municipality of Finland located on the shore of the Gulf of Finland; it is the seat of the region information. I define it this way, HELL-sinking. Why meet in Finland, a sinking, hopeless place and toxic cave of existence, pulling Trump right into it along with Putin, a former KGB agent, alone without an interpreter. Putin put in all his demands and requests. Suspicious of the disservice Trump did by this meeting was not smart on his part, because he was weak and Putin knows how he changes, lies, and flip flops, completely degrading others. Putin took advantage of him. It was a calculated risk on Trump's part. He also took the soccer ball Putin gave him and when the reporter asked Putin did he want Trump to win, he stated that he did. The reporter also asked Putin if he gave compromising information about Trump, which he would not answer directly.

What does Putin really have on him? Why did Trump want to meet with him without his ambassador or his translator? And what did Putin dictate to Trump? Why was GOP not concerned? The tale of two evils, scheming and guarding their well-kept secrets. When and how their plan will come to light, Trump returned from the meeting with a pumped-up head wanting a parade and acting like a dictator. Trump stated that his relationship with Russia "has never been worse". He also said Putin was "okay" and that he loved Kim Jung Un. He sided with Putin over his own intelligence agencies and Cabinet members. Also just a reminder, Putin showed up 45 minutes late for this meeting. Trump refuses to hold Putin accountable for his wrongdoings. Then Trump began to complain about the FBI and the Special Counsel, the DOJ, and the CIA. One could surmise that Putin laid ground rules by telling Trump he was in charge and in control of the U.S. and that he had the power to change and make laws. Trump is just a game of cards with bad tricks and different suits.

From the beginning, Trump made a point of tweeting that he was the real deal. However, all his cards were on the table. But Trump playing his Trump card is not a winning hand. Game after game, as he picks from the deck, he could not give himself a win or develop into a ranking hand with Putin or Kim Jung Un, who were walking away from the deal. Believing what they say, "the definition of a Trump Card is a winning card". The "card" he referred to is a set of proposals within laws passed that will benefit the welfare of our nation's citizens. In other words, you will play by Trump's hand. Also, they were warned not to follow Trump along the rabbit trail or down the rabbit hole.

# CHAPTER THREE

# America is Under Attack from Within

The parties are constantly fighting among each other. Trump is warring with his own Cabinet and he has no concern and no responsibility, no duties of his office, no skills. He is blowing it, calling Kim Jung Un a little rocket man. He continues to spend his time tweeting and criticizing, name-calling, instead of taking care of more important issues. He slanders, calling people dogs and sons of bitches. Evangelical pastors and others continue to defend him, as he continues to craft lies and cause unrest. It is dangerous to continue to incite riots and not realize the harm and pain it is causing. Putin is not playing Russian Roulette with Trump, he is serious. It is not a game but he is enjoying all the news he hears about Trump. He has done a lot of damage to hurt the USA. And then he brings Rudy Giuliani into the picture, who said that the truth is not the truth. He is gambling with Trump's life. This should be an eye-opener for Trump to see Giuliani engaged in mudding the water and playing with the justice system.

Even though Trump also ran his campaign on "Build that Wall" and stated that Mexico would pay for that wall, he still finds himself behind many walls of grotesque tweets. He is also allowed to get away with unfair attacks on women. The situation he is in provides a glass wall where his dirty secrets and scandals are plastered and his enormous amount of personal affairs have been aired. The dirt keeps looming over him and his so-called friends are beginning to turn on him. There is also a laundry list, the tabloid safe opening, the *National Enquire* holding some of his secrets. The imaginary wall being built by Trump is giving the whole world a grandeur view of his illusion and lot of his exaggerations, but no freedom will settle his optimistic ideas on his unimaged talking points that there is no colluding. Yes, a wall for protection against his constant attacks on women and on the Democrats. The freedom of speech will doom over his mouth for decades due to his lies, and his attacks of the press and it will not be "fake news". The heart of America is under siege from within. Damage control continues to level insults and division by one individual who allows the master of demise who is Putin to divide the American people.

Only a higher power can work this nation's heart of the matter with laws governed to protect us as citizens; which is our freedom as well as our peace. But we hold these truths to be self-evident: that all men are created equal; that they are endowed by their creator with certain unalienable rights. That among these are life, liberty, and the pursuit of happiness is to secure "rights, and government" that are instituted among men deriving just power from the consent, therefore, that all men are created equal.

# CHAPTER FOUR

# Truth is Generally the Best Vindication Against Lies and Slander

Building a wall has leveled many disputes. Number one, why America is not made great again. Because America is at an all-time low and worse than ever, stirring up hate with white supremacy and other white nationalists. On "Draining of the Swamp", there have been more swamp critters than ever in American history to hurt, destroy, and racially divide the American people. There are many of Trump's puppets patrolling the world staging lies. Someone stated that "lies never die and will continue to creep up in your life after you are gone".

Truth, on the other hand, will end, and the effects it has on your past can change your future and it can make your free. The wall that Trump wants to build is somehow closing in on him and will fall on him and crush him to pieces. Someone has stated that President Trump will go down in history as one of the worst presidents. He has a lot of hostility toward Hillary Clinton, President Obama and he cannot bring himself to consult with formal presidents. We often see a violence temper displayed and names calling, displaying of the Illuminati signs. His imperfections are not hidden, they are out in the open, and his arrogance some have said is "intangible".

The Republicans refuse to take a stand and call out Trump's many faults and this is problematic. It unimaginable that he can get away with so many lies and to have such a following when he is a danger to our democracy and to our country. He is letting the country down. He refuses to change his attitude toward Russia and hate groups. This is troubling and unsettling. He has gained the reputation as the payback President. He also dismisses people that speak out against him. Some are afraid of him and refuse to call him out when he lies. There are only a few who are not afraid, even though they are retiring. He is waking up a host of sleeping giants and haters—his rallies stir up hate.

He is a thief, stealing the American dream more than any foreign adversary ever could. And the House and Senate are not of any help in allowing their own party to be destroyed. They are not concerned about the scandals hanging over the White House – the more than 4,000 lies and 17 female accusers. Many of his Cabinet members have shady pasts and are causing some upset. They have crossed the line so many times. Corruption continues to gloom over the white house and some of the GOP. They know he is guilty of obstruction and trying to impede the investigation by Mueller, it has been said if he was innocent, he would not try to get rid of those doing the investigation. If Obama committed just one of these offenses he would have been impeached. Trump's team does not realize that Putin has gotten to him. Mitch McConnell and Paul Ryan are not functional as a governing body of the House and Senate. A toxic wave of evil and shame brought about with the shady business dealings with Russia, dark secrets under the presumptuous role of Rudy Giuliani, the fixer, and members of his party should be exploding.

# CHAPTER FIVE

# CLOUDS OVER THE WHITE HOUSE

Paul Ryan and Mitch McConnell are betraying the American people by not keeping tabs and checks and balances on the lawmaking process as framed in the Constitution of the United States. Someone stated that, "it took an internal group to come out of hiding to do Mitch McConnell and Paul Ryan job". Neglecting the American people for the big buck lobbyists and rich donors have attracted others to defend and dismiss the wrongdoings of Trump. The Russian probe brought to the forefront Nunes and his group. Trump is the subject in the Russian investigation, and he continued to wage war on those that spoke out against him, and he continues to commit obstruction of justice. He said it was something he had to do, question what he means. But first, he is in denial, calling the Russian investigation a "witch hunt", insisting there is "no collusion", and firing Comey. His conduct is saying otherwise.

He looks for loyalty from the government workers to pay homage to him. Trump said keeping the Russians out is the purpose of the statement he made on July 11, 2018, publicly about Germany. The decision to buy massive amounts of gas from Russia. NATO is not Germany's concern any longer. Trump also remarked that we are protecting Germany, France, and other countries that formed to keep Russia out (giving Putin a voice). He should not be allowed to give bad advice. Even though he thinks "no one knows the system better than" him.

Trump finally admits that his campaign colluded with Russia at the Trump Tower meeting and that Russia helped him steal the election of 2016. He said, Russia, if you are listening, find Hillary's emails. GOP are you listening? Are you doing fact-checking?

# CHAPTER SIX

# WHY TRUMP USED THE WORD TREASON

When Trump heard the word treason spoken, he attacked Brennon and the news media, having no idea and no understanding of its meaning as it was leveled against him. He in turn revoked clearance of CIA and other former agents. And he continues to tweet, not realizing that there are thousands of pieces of evidence of what he has said. He has no understanding of what he is doing. Why continue to tweet and praise himself, this does not display humanity or respect. In order to know the ins and outs of how the government should be run takes responsibility and respectability and accepting advice from those who have worked for the government for years with past knowledge and experience. It should be noted there are consequences to our doing, with the moral character of kindness to be shown.

The Trump administration has been marked by a series of exits from high ranking officials' appointments expected to last for years have only made it a matter of days ending in chaotic departures. An analysis of the rate of departures by the Brookins Institution found that the Trump turnover is higher than five previous presidents. "The resigned and the ones he fired are about thirty-nine and counting." His turnover administration and unprecedented misleading claims in 558 days is 5,000 lies and counting, 30,000 tweets, and about 487 name-callings and insults. The GOP just got nasty and dirty working overtime spreading lies and fear in voting purging.

"Over the course of 21 months, President Trump has loudly and repletely refused to accept a number of seemingly agreed upon facts, while insisting on the veracity of a variety of demonstrably false claims that happen to suit his political needs."

"Trump vs. reality without saying a 'LIE', *New York Times* writer Maggie Haberman shows the way and proved her chops by writing an entire article about Donald Trump's habitual rejections of truth without using the word 'LIE' (1300 words) a president who believes he is entitled to his own facts."

Trump often fires Cabinet members, that do not agree with him. He constantly tweets his disagreements and criticism and name-calling. He has no knowledge of the Constitution or government procedures. He does not take responsibilities on the more important issues. His lack of abilities and skills are devastating to our country. The "TFA" and "Op/Ed statement" should have awakened him to realize the clouds hanging over the White House were of a serious nature and a wake-up call. Anonymously and secretive of those working against him was not done cowardly but in fear. No one came forward or owned up to it did not want their heads rolling off by Trump's theft and slandering. He has brought out evil and a lot of animosity in a group of haters and racial division. Much of his base are those who continue to harbor those feelings and beliefs within themselves. The White supremacy has a belief that they are superior over others. Nationalists believe in advocating for political independence for their country. Trump continues his crusade and attack on the press. He continues to float out lies.

# CHAPTER SEVEN

# Attacks and Coverups

Trump attacking the press and Mueller and his talk of no collusion. Threats of firing Sessions and Rosenstein as he has fired Comey and McCabe, threats also continue against the CIA, DOJ, and FBI. The GOP has turned a deaf ear and are working to keep Trump in the office but are showing heartless care for the USA by allowing him to continue to destroy and disrupt as he remains in office. They also ignore the obstruction so they can carry out what they deem important, no matter how many lawsuits are leveled against him. He has turned against U.S. allies and continues to blame everyone except himself. He has become so unstable, unsettling, vindictive and contradicting. His misleading statements are full of propaganda, so consumed with hate for the Democrats, smear tactics continue to surface about fake news. Only *Fox News* he deems as real.

# CHAPTER EIGHT

# The Term Drain the Swamp

Trump used the metaphor to describe his plan to fix the problem in the federal government as "honest" and again he vowed that he would take on the "power" structure in Washington and "drain" the swamp of all the lobbyists who contributed to hurt the working class. Note this phrase or term alludes the training of draining the swamp to keep mosquito population low in why Trump could not just be the President of the United States of America instead of a troublesome adversary, why he was not truthful, honest, and most importantly trustworthy.

The way it all unfolded; thirty-five members working in his Cabinet were terminated or brought up on federal charges. Trump thought that every secret he had was locked in Pecker vaults and still he has not learned his lesson. Therefore, there are statements after statements with putting America first. He continues to put himself first and that is downright unrighteous.

Let the truth be told. The ways of his reckless behavior add to his conspiracies and continue to be leveled every day, which he blames shift and the silent war that is prevalent as the talking points echo in Americans' ears. In addition, this nation faces danger every day, which imposes scandals and violence, and on top of that, there is chaos in this land. Everything Trump has promised and continues to promise fails. The damage is done as well as it is felt.

"The myth of Trump" is unraveling and his wall of lies, secrecy is eroding and growing legal challenges. However, "former Trump supporters are speaking out after learning the MAGA cult. A dictator in the White House has surrounded himself with crooks". He is classified as being an antagonist or a narcissist. His characteristics from the beginning is of the "religious right", besides his dirty mouth, bullying, and adulterous ways, make these offices a religious shame, blamed on the Democrats, which is detached from reality.

Mountains of books are written about his many flaws, lies, chaos, and his tweets. His mixups, twisting of the truth, secrets, Op/Ed: anonymous, and continuation of showing favoritism to foreign leaders. Extending an invite to Putin in order to visit Washington D.C. in 2019. Trump changed his mind at the secret meeting between himself and Putin behind closed doors, which will continue to be a reminder for the American population. Signals just keep coming from Putin:

1.  Withdrawal from Syria.
2.  The missile.
3.  An invitation to Turkey.
4.  Trump thanked Saudi Arabia.

When the facts are hidden in the shadow quotes from local officials are hidden. The sound of Trump will doom over America including attacks on institutions, the very fabrications of what our government stands for, and silent blows toward the DOJ, FBI, and CIA. It is in Trump's makeup to choose to fight against righteous indignation, and it shows where his heart and mind is and in actuality, it is not with America.

# CHAPTER NINE

# Witch Hunt

The witches are not riding on broomsticks, they are flying very high and sweeping up more dirt, more scandals, more trouble for Trump. Why does Trump use these phrases so often? The dictionary says that It's a search for and subsequent persecution of a supposed witch informal—it is a campaign directed against a person or group holding unorthodox views. Merriam Webster definition is a search out for persecution of individuals accused of witchcraft. Searching out and deliberate harassment of those political opponents with unpopular views. It is also an attempt to find and punish suspected characters of action.

On July 31, 2015, then presidential candidate Trump said publicly, "I think I would get along well with Putin." In October, he repeated, "I think I would get along with Putin very well." In U.S. history, there has never been such a love relationship with Putin until Trump came along. President Trump and Putin have formed a relationship. It is from "Russia with love". Fact checks are needed for meeting with Putin. It appears Trump as President of the United States is abandoning our traditional Western Allies and siding instead with Putin and Russia. Collusion is deeper and dirtier than we know. Just weeks into Trump's presidency, his National Security Advisor, Michael Flynn, the most pro-Russian adviser was fired. The U.S. said it would not end sanctions on Russia and that it expects Russia to return Crimea to Ukraine. Right out of the playbook of Putin and Kim Jung Un, Trump has become so intoxicated with imitation of those who dictate, that he himself is acting like a dictator. He continues to call the Russian probe a witch hunt, but he continues to do Putin's bidding—pulling out of Syria and blaming the Democrats for shutting down the government. Even though he said himself he would take the blame for the shutdown.

Immigrationdetachmentisheartbreaking—snatching children out of their mothers' arms and putting them on lockdown in cages. Yet, he has some other immigrants working at the golf course and he has undocumented illegal immigrants unaccounted for. Concealed and undocumented workers while he talked about how they entered the country, became criminals, and took American jobs away from the American people. Note: the American people will not do the job the immigrants do for a lower wage, but Trump proposes immigration deals in a bid to end the shutdown. According to the headlines report, President Trump's golf club concealed undocumented workers and was busted for giving out fake green cards to undocumented workers.

# CHAPTER TEN

# Trump's War on Democrats

Trump's war on the Democrats is an all-out fabrication, the very things he accuses the Democrats of are untrue, and his lies always contradicts the truth. In his first year as president, there were 2,140 to 4,229 false and misleading claims. He is using unethical and illegal campaign practices and attacking the Democrats with poisonous words and untruthful statements and more lies. The attack and dimension of one's reputation without respect and the characterization of untruth. But it is worse pointing the finger at the Democrats when Trump all along is spreading derogatory remarks. Also, he uses crooked, dishonest smear tactics, causing him to lose respect based on his own lies, which contribute to his own self-assassination.

# CHAPTER ELEVEN

# All the World's a
# Centerfold Stage

Jacques speaking his famous phrase, "As you like it". "All the world's a stage". Right from the start, Trump's life was played out on stage in the open. He made statements, but one that stood out the most was by Billy Bush. Trump stated that he could grab women by their private parts, bragging vulgar words and having zero respect for women and women's rights. There are nineteen sexual misconduct accusers, whom his lewd comments took this to a whole new level. All a while he was hiding behind lies and parading as well as campaigning a big circus act. Subsequently, he was clowning, calling women names.

Actually, Trump's world is like a stage show. He has his entrances and strategies of exiting away from the crowd who happen to be bystanders. There are no metaphorical messages behind his life. He is an imagining, personification of grand ideas, of being the clown who is best at babbling and repeating words out of his own playbook as a distraction. Everyone must play by his set of rules.

Many of his actions make him feel as if he is above the law. His mind frame makes him think that people in this country should pay homage to him. If that does not happen, there is hell to pay. In addition, he tweets, he has melt-downs, and he flips out. He does not stick with the truth. He berates into orbit with an epic fury which causes rage. His lies, that again baffles, fake news turns into fact-checking, which calls him out on his lies. It is difficult for him to refer to what he previously said from the beginning of his statements, and he seems to forget what he has said in general.

You cannot pivot from the sound of the last Trump rant. Vibrations will continue to travel through the airing of the news channels and statements made by the press and the population of the people.

Just to key in, Dr. Murrell stated at the meeting on August 1, 2018, with the Pastors. Pastor Scott and other Evangelicals should have done their homework before you start praising this president. A religious one just does your homework! But President Trump's policies on ethical community and marginalizing population, voter purging, rampant mass incarnation on Blacks, and instructing his Attorney General Jeff Sessions to revitalize the war on drugs. His nominees of eighty-seven court appointees, eighty-five being White, just one Black, and one Hispanic.

On the other hand, Senator McCain's farewell message warned against TRUMPISM. He said we weaken America when we hide behind walls. We will get through these troublesome times. Warning of confusing PATRIOTISM with TRIBAL RIVALRIES. McCain said he learned to love his country while in captivity. He was beaten every two to four hours for two-thousand and eight days. He withstood harsh treatment and was kept in solitary confinement for years.

During Trump's speech he failed to name him on August 14, 2018, even when the bill signing was intended to honor the dying senator. Trump finally said he respected McCain's "service to the country" when asked by a reporter, and then went silent before ending the conversation by saying, "thank you, thank you, thank you". McCain was a great American hero who served for thirty-one years. Someone stated that, "McCain was just a thorn in Trump's side" and is everything that Trump is not.

# CHAPTER TWELVE

# Facts and Hearing

Trump has been referred to as a "BLOWHARD" by President G.W.H. Bush. He boasts about his accomplishments and does so in a systematically and obnoxious and unpleasant way, claiming credit for others' accomplishments. He constantly talks about what he has done, things that no one else has ever done. Trump said he was thankful for himself on Thanksgiving. He boasts about the size of the crowd at his rallies. He loves to be the center of attention, loves to take center stage and declare victories on all front. I think that President G.W.H. Bush hit the nail on it—BLOWHARD. He often puts himself first, and we cannot move forward with putting America first or making America great again because Trump is making himself great. He rages and rants about everyone and everything. He has tarnished his own reputation.

French President Macron warned against NATIONALISM and PATRIOTISM and rebuilding Trump's policies. He responded to Trump tweets, telling him he does not do policy or diplomacy by tweets or Twitter, and declining to lash out. Instead, taking the long view and making it clear that he was not going to respond in kind, but rather show both countries' longstanding common interests.

Even George Conway weighed in, Kellyanne Conway's husband. He said he would rather go to some beach in Australia than to vote for Trump. He was deeply offended by the way Trump attacked the Justice Department. The Republican Party has become a personality cult under Trump. Trump is all about himself. This is dividing its own party and the result is Congress gets worse as the party follows Trump right over the cliff. And his war on women has brought many women to the forefront or into Congress.

# CHAPTER THIRTEEN

# Sadly

Finally, there is going to be the sound of the last trumpet. It will be turned into weeping and gnashing of teeth and casting out into darkness and into a furnace of fire much wailing and tearing in His wrath, haters, hypocritical mockers, liars, evildoers, and many workers of iniquity. For God Himself shall descend from Heaven with a SHOUT with the voice of the Archangel and with the TRIUMPH OF GOD. But of the times and seasons, for you yourselves know perfectly that the day of the Lord cometh as a thief in the night, and when they shall say peace and safety; then sudden destruction cometh upon them and they shall not escape. I am urgent for the expectancy plus endurance. But regrettable how we cannot make a distinction, not realizing how important it is to be ready.

Politicians must reiterate and make a distinction and must be held accountable to those elected to represent the people for their behavior regarding the election that should be reserved for those who recognize human identity. An echo of valve and trust placed in them must be characterized. Their ideologies of politics have moved to dirty tricks, lies, and dirty changes. However, all respects and opinions have erupted; after they were elected. Evil heart and black soul of politics will change for the big bucks, lobbying and division will surface. There should be just one party. The future of tomorrow's ways of campaigning is tarnished. The White House has changed since the 2008 year of President Obama. Racism has escalated and will continue to have consequences. There are two world views of politics that has infiltrated into our government and reaped "havoc", therefore, it is no greater value including atrocities, counterfeits with scapegoats, as well as chaos in today's society.

The precious things in life are not or should not be taken for granted no matter what choices we choose or make, or how we live our lives. We need to move forward and be unbiased to the real facts of life. Precious things cannot be lofted in hate and lies. They must be gained and kept and inspired. "Lying to win or cheating is not a lasting hope." Just imagine later on in life when we come to realize the many lies and mistakes that drove us to commit falsehood, agreeing with Trump and his lies, never realizing the harm and damage caused by him inciting his base, his abuse of power and his selfishness, and representing himself and not the American people.

One day his secrets will be founded out and revealed and they will destroy him and his children along with the GOP. There will be consequences after consequences, and possibly a great price for the hurt and turmoil caused for all the missing children snatched from the arms of their parent. The facts remain, God of this world will judge the wickedness and the evil doers.

# CHAPTER FOURTEEN

# "Guilty by Association and Design"

Whether there is a law on this particular topic, words should be spoken more carefully instead of being careless, passive instead of active, and not viral. Human individuals are more inclined to accept what leaders say. Leaders will be able to act without restrictions. However, there were statements made against the press and the Democrats and other people without proof, solely for reasons unknown but as a result in attribution leveled up against them. I have taken note of these views very carefully. And not to say it carelessly "guilty by association and design" has caused many attacks with the government and on individuals mentioned solely by the president doing his televised speeches. For instance, pipe bombs sent to seventeen of Trump's critics such as Cesar Sayoc who became a suspect that was lost and angry. The group was not taking Trump speeches literally, they were taken "outlawed".

A Coast Guard officer compiled a list of about twenty Democratic journalists. White Supremacist Christopher Paul Hasson at the age of forty-nine was charged with planning a mass attack, targeting Democrats and

Journalist who had a thousand round of ammunition, then drafted an email that stated, "I am dreaming of a way to kill almost every last person on the earth. I think a plague would be most successful, but how do I acquire the needed Spanish Flu, botulism, anthrax; not sure yet but something interesting can start with biological attack followed by major food supply."

However, not all people who commit these crimes know much about politics. President Trump is one of the worst presidents of our time. Not in a million years can we find worse than we have now. Currently, there is an economic human crisis with parent and child separation. ("Blame is on both sides, there is good and bad on both sides.") It has been noted that he is dangerous. How much more evidence do we need other than his racial bias and money-making deals?

# CHAPTER FIFTEEN

# No Holds Barr

William P. Barr, 85th U.S. Attorney General and an American attorney who previously served as the 77th A.G. from 1991 to 1993 under the Bush Administration was a member of the Republican Party B.D. as well as A.J.D. He was born in 1950 and is now age sixty-eight. Trump decided to bring Barr on even though there are many "red flags" being raised about Barr's prior statement mentioned and his "resume" had many fabricated wrinkles to be ironed out. He is an extremist. Trump has looked for the resumes of lawyers who criticized the Mueller Investigation and has weighed in on the statement they made regarding a sitting President who does not qualify to be indicted; same with the Kavanaugh statement and Whitaker. Katie Banner said William P. Barr must tell Congress why the Special Counsel work concluded. But he was not legally obligated to provide full detail of the report (even with all of the previous arrests of Trump association and the firing whom he wanted someone to not rescue them self). When will there be a "Constitution Person", says someone who cares about the truth instead of Trumpism?

More mistakes resulting from a combination of words used "should" or "could" would have been avoided on speeches said in the form of evil expressions. Jeff Sessions

III is an American politician and lawyer who served as the 84th U.S. Attorney General from 2017 through 2018. He was a Republican Senator from Alabama from 1977 to 2017 and resigned from the position to serve in the Trump Administration.

For two years, the *Washington Post*, *The New York Times*, *MSNBC*, and *CNN* observed—Mueller is a hero and the Mueller report that his time and experience with Trump administration has been a historic time in our government. The aftermath is sending shock waves to some and doubt to many, contradicting the outcome of the American people who have a right to know that the Mueller Report is a key part of knowing his recommendation and whether there has been a violation of our Constitution. However, new political battles are ahead because the indictments infuriated Trump and threw his administration into turmoil.

## Political Laws Are Changing
### The worst kind of campaigning.

The defining moment in our politics with scheming and escalation of division. There's one word with so many synonyms that describes our time in history with the attack on the FBI, DOJ, CIA . . .

REPUGNANT actions are defining and hovering over our government and the behavior of the Trump team is becoming unpleasant causing a feeling of disgust, distaste, objection, offense, and unacceptable conflict. I have never known of such word with so much meaning to characterize and describe the GOP in our history until now. Synonyms of repugnant: abhorrent, revolting, repulsive, repellant, disgusting, offensive, objectionable, vile, nasty attitude, scheming, hateful, monstrous, appalling, deplorable, reprehensible, intolerable, contemptable, and disagreeable. The Republicans standing with Trump in his lies and crime is repugnant. Our constitution must not be changed by Trump.

TRUMPSY, GRUMPSY JUST STUMPSY LIKE
HUMPTY DUMPTY
TRYING TO SIT ON THAT WALL, TRYING TO
SIT ON THAT WALL

JUST LIKE HUMPTY DUMPTY
TRUMPSY GRUMPSY TOOK A GREAT FALL
TOOK A GREAT FALL

TRUMPSY GRUMPSY KEEP DUMPING AND DUMPING
AND CAN'T INSTALL
HE CAN'T INSTALL, HE CAN'T MAKE THAT CALL

TRUMPSY GRUMPSY AIN'T HIP AT ALL,
HE AIN'T HIP AT ALL

TRUMPSY GRUMPSY YOU CAN'T BUILD THAT WALL,
YOU CAN'T BUILD THAT WALL

TRUMPSY GRUMPSY STUMPING AND
GRUMPING AND DUMPING
LIKE HUMPTY DUMPTY YOU CAN'T INSTALL
YOU CAN'T INSTALL, YOU CAN'T BUILD THAT WALL

www.ingramcontent.com/pod-product-compliance
Lightning Source LLC
Chambersburg PA
CBHW051423250726
48655CB00003B/1199